Reptiles

Written by Sarah O'Neil

sundance

There are many different reptiles.
Lizards are reptiles.
Turtles are reptiles.
Snakes are reptiles.
Crocodiles are reptiles, too.

All reptiles have a skeleton
inside their body.

This is a snake's skeleton.

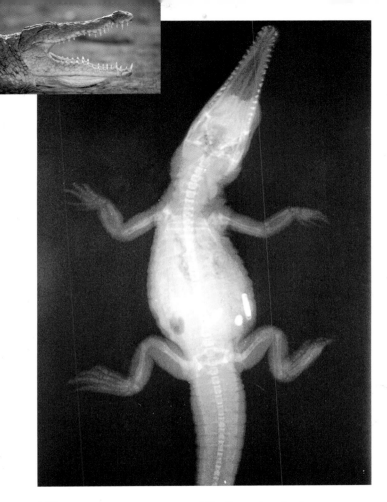

This is a crocodile's skeleton.

All reptiles are cold-blooded.
They cannot make body heat.

This snake gets warm
by lying in the sun.

This alligator is lying in the sun
to get warm, too.

All reptiles have scales on their skin.

As some reptiles grow bigger,
they grow a new skin
and shed their old skin.

This snake is shedding
its old skin.

Most reptiles lay eggs.

This turtle is hatching
from an egg.

This snake is hatching
from an egg.

Most reptiles eat other animals.
Some reptiles eat only plants.

This lizard is eating an insect.

This turtle is eating a plant.

Reptiles can be many colors.

This lizard is gray.

This lizard is green and white.

Index